Off The Leash
DIARY **2017**

Rupert Fawcett

F
FRANCES
LINCOLN

Moon Phases
- ● New Moon
- ☽ First Quarter
- ○ Full Moon
- ☾ Last Quarter

Frances Lincoln Limited
www.quartoknows.com

Off the Leash Diary 2017
Copyright © Frances Lincoln Limited 2016
Illustrations copyright © Rupert Fawcett 2016
Off the Leash copyright © Rupert Fawcett 2016
Licensed by Clive Juster & Associates

First Frances Lincoln edition 2016

Every effort is made to ensure calendarial data is correct at the time of going to press but the publisher cannot accept any liability for any errors or changes.

All rights reserved. No part of this publication may be reproduced, stored in a retrieval system or transmitted, in any form, or by any means, electronic, mechanical, photocopying, recording or otherwise, without either prior permission in writing from the publishers or a licence permitting restricted copying. In the United Kingdom such licences are issued by the Copyright Licensing Agency, Barnard's Inn, 86 Fetter Lane, London, EC4A 1EN.

A catalogue record for this book is available from the British Library

978-0-7112-3797-1
Printed in China

9 8 7 6 5 4 3 2 1

Off The Leash Find us on **Facebook**

CALENDAR **2017**

JANUARY
M T W T F S S
          1
2 3 4 5 6 7 8
9 10 11 12 13 14 15
16 17 18 19 20 21 22
23 24 25 26 27 28 29
30 31

FEBRUARY
M T W T F S S
    1 2 3 4 5
6 7 8 9 10 11 12
13 14 15 16 17 18 19
20 21 22 23 24 25 26
27 28

MARCH
M T W T F S S
    1 2 3 4 5
6 7 8 9 10 11 12
13 14 15 16 17 18 19
20 21 22 23 24 25 26
27 28 29 30 31

APRIL
M T W T F S S
          1 2
3 4 5 6 7 8 9
10 11 12 13 14 15 16
17 18 19 20 21 22 23
24 25 26 27 28 29 30

MAY
M T W T F S S
1 2 3 4 5 6 7
8 9 10 11 12 13 14
15 16 17 18 19 20 21
22 23 24 25 26 27 28
29 30 31

JUNE
M T W T F S S
      1 2 3 4
5 6 7 8 9 10 11
12 13 14 15 16 17 18
19 20 21 22 23 24 25
26 27 28 29 30

JULY
M T W T F S S
          1 2
3 4 5 6 7 8 9
10 11 12 13 14 15 16
17 18 19 20 21 22 23
24 25 26 27 28 29 30
31

AUGUST
M T W T F S S
  1 2 3 4 5 6
7 8 9 10 11 12 13
14 15 16 17 18 19 20
21 22 23 24 25 26 27
28 29 30 31

SEPTEMBER
M T W T F S S
        1 2 3
4 5 6 7 8 9 10
11 12 13 14 15 16 17
18 19 20 21 22 23 24
25 26 27 28 29 30

OCTOBER
M T W T F S S
            1
2 3 4 5 6 7 8
9 10 11 12 13 14 15
16 17 18 19 20 21 22
23 24 25 26 27 28 29
30 31

NOVEMBER
M T W T F S S
    1 2 3 4 5
6 7 8 9 10 11 12
13 14 15 16 17 18 19
20 21 22 23 24 25 26
27 28 29 30

DECEMBER
M T W T F S S
        1 2 3
4 5 6 7 8 9 10
11 12 13 14 15 16 17
18 19 20 21 22 23 24
25 26 27 28 29 30 31

CALENDAR **2018**

JANUARY
M T W T F S S
1 2 3 4 5 6 7
8 9 10 11 12 13 14
15 16 17 18 19 20 21
22 23 24 25 26 27 28
29 30 31

FEBRUARY
M T W T F S S
      1 2 3 4
5 6 7 8 9 10 11
12 13 14 15 16 17 18
19 20 21 22 23 24 25
26 27 28

MARCH
M T W T F S S
      1 2 3 4
5 6 7 8 9 10 11
12 13 14 15 16 17 18
19 20 21 22 23 24 25
26 27 28 29 30 31

APRIL
M T W T F S S
            1
2 3 4 5 6 7 8
9 10 11 12 13 14 15
16 17 18 19 20 21 22
23 24 25 26 27 28 29
30

MAY
M T W T F S S
  1 2 3 4 5 6
7 8 9 10 11 12 13
14 15 16 17 18 19 20
21 22 23 24 25 26 27
28 29 30 31

JUNE
M T W T F S S
        1 2 3
4 5 6 7 8 9 10
11 12 13 14 15 16 17
18 19 20 21 22 23 24
25 26 27 28 29 30

JULY
M T W T F S S
            1
2 3 4 5 6 7 8
9 10 11 12 13 14 15
16 17 18 19 20 21 22
23 24 25 26 27 28 29
30 31

AUGUST
M T W T F S S
    1 2 3 4 5
6 7 8 9 10 11 12
13 14 15 16 17 18 19
20 21 22 23 24 25 26
27 28 29 30 31

SEPTEMBER
M T W T F S S
          1 2
3 4 5 6 7 8 9
10 11 12 13 14 15 16
17 18 19 20 21 22 23
24 25 26 27 28 29 30

OCTOBER
M T W T F S S
1 2 3 4 5 6 7
8 9 10 11 12 13 14
15 16 17 18 19 20 21
22 23 24 25 26 27 28
29 30 31

NOVEMBER
M T W T F S S
      1 2 3 4
5 6 7 8 9 10 11
12 13 14 15 16 17 18
19 20 21 22 23 24 25
26 27 28 29 30

DECEMBER
M T W T F S S
          1 2
3 4 5 6 7 8 9
10 11 12 13 14 15 16
17 18 19 20 21 22 23
24 25 26 27 28 29 30
31

PERSONAL DETAILS

name..
home address...
....
....

telephone..
mobile..
e-mail...

....
work address..
....
....

telephone..
mobile..
e-mail...
website..
other info..
....
....
....
....
....
....
....
....
....
....
....
....
....

LIZZIE DIDN'T HAVE A LOT OF EXCITEMENT IN HER LIFE, BUT SHE DID HAVE THE POSTMAN

DECEMBER/JANUARY • WEEK 52

monday
26

Boxing Day (St Stephen's Day)
Holiday, UK, Republic of Ireland, Canada,
Australia and New Zealand

tuesday
27

Holiday, UK, Australia and New Zealand

wednesday
28

thursday
29

●

friday
30

saturday
31

New Year's Eve

sunday
1

New Year's Day

JANUARY

M	T	W	T	F	S	S
						1
2	3	4	5	6	7	8
9	10	11	12	13	14	15
16	17	18	19	20	21	22
23	24	25	26	27	28	29
30	31					

JANUARY • WEEK 1

monday 2 — Holiday, UK, Republic of Ireland, USA, Canada, Australia and New Zealand

tuesday 3 — Holiday, Scotland and New Zealand
K back to work, kids back to school. Dentist 9.30, polled out broken part of tooth + built up remains. Fingers X'd it stays.

wednesday 4

thursday 5
Out to Tindle with Anne + Judith. Cold but sunny. Missy ok in cage but hyper this afternoon. 2 short walks + garden time

friday 6 — Epiphany
Little walk in the rain. Better on lead Cold showery, milder + rain later

saturday 7
Sunny mild

sunday 8

HERE WE GO... A NEW KEEP FIT CAMPAIGN...
'RUNNING THE DOG INSTEAD OF WALKING THE DOG'...
NEW TRAINERS, NEW LYCRA PANTS, NEW SPORTS BRA, FANCY PINK HAND-WEIGHTS...
...I GIVE IT A WEEK.
RF

JANUARY · WEEK 2

monday
9

tuesday
10

wednesday
11

○

thursday
12

friday
13

saturday
14

sunday
15

JANUARY

M T W T F S S
              1
2 3 4 5 6 7 8
9 10 11 12 13 14 15
16 17 18 19 20 21 22
23 24 25 26 27 28 29
30 31

JANUARY · WEEK 3

monday
16

Holiday, USA (Martin Luther King Jnr Day)

tuesday
17

wednesday
18

thursday
19

☾

friday
20

saturday
21

sunday
22

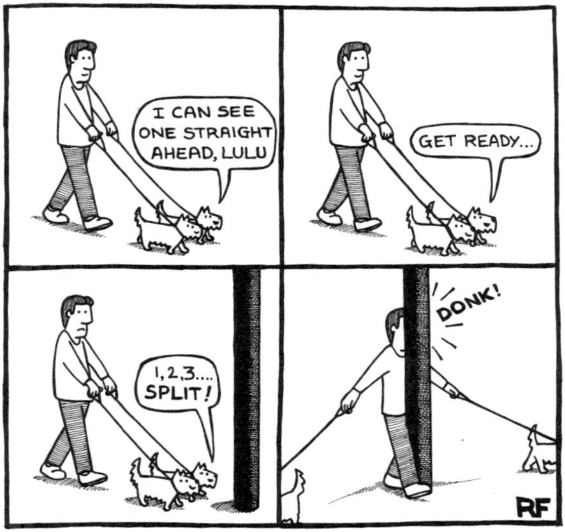
I CAN SEE ONE STRAIGHT AHEAD, LULU
GET READY...
1,2,3.... SPLIT!
DONK!
RF

JANUARY · WEEK 4

monday
23

tuesday
24

wednesday
25

thursday
26

Holiday, Australia (Australia Day)

friday
27

saturday
28

Chinese New Year ●

sunday
29

JANUARY

M	T	W	T	F	S	S
						1
2	3	4	5	6	7	8
9	10	11	12	13	14	15
16	17	18	19	20	21	22
23	24	25	26	27	28	29
30	31					

JANUARY/FEBRUARY • WEEK 5

monday
30

tuesday
31

wednesday
1

thursday
2

friday
3

saturday
4

☽

sunday
5

OOH, LOOK AT THE GOLDEN RETRIEVERS WITH THEIR BIG TAILS, SWISH, SWISH, SWISH!
YEAH, SWISH, SWISH, SWISH, ALL HIGH AND MIGHTY!
MUMMY, WHAT ARE THOSE DOGS SAYING?
IGNORE THEM SWEETIE, IT'S JUST TAIL-ENVY
RF

FEBRUARY · WEEK 6

monday
6

Accession of Queen Elizabeth II
Holiday, New Zealand (Waitangi Day)

tuesday
7

wednesday
8

thursday
9

friday
10

saturday
11

○

sunday
12

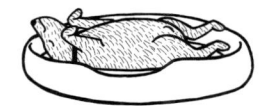

FEBRUARY

M	T	W	T	F	S	S
		1	2	3	4	5
6	7	8	9	10	11	12
13	14	15	16	17	18	19
20	21	22	23	24	25	26
27	28					

FEBRUARY • WEEK 7

monday
13

tuesday
14
Valentine's Day

wednesday
15

thursday
16

friday
17

saturday
18
☾

sunday
19

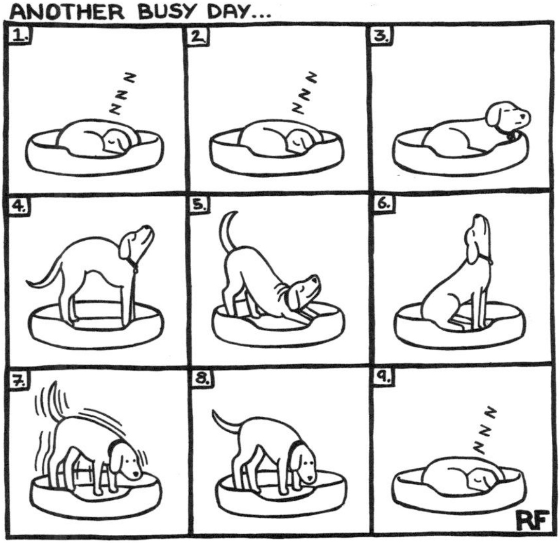
ANOTHER BUSY DAY...
1.
2.
3.
4.
5.
6.
7.
8.
9.
RF

FEBRUARY · WEEK 8

Holiday, USA (Presidents' Day)

monday
20

tuesday
21

wednesday
22

thursday
23

friday
24

saturday
25

sunday
26

FEBRUARY

M	T	W	T	F	S	S
		1	2	3	4	5
6	7	8	9	10	11	12
13	14	15	16	17	18	19
20	21	22	23	24	25	26
27	28					

FEBRUARY/MARCH • WEEK 9

monday
27

tuesday
28

Shrove Tuesday

wednesday
1

St David's Day
Ash Wednesday

thursday
2

friday
3

saturday
4

sunday
5

☽

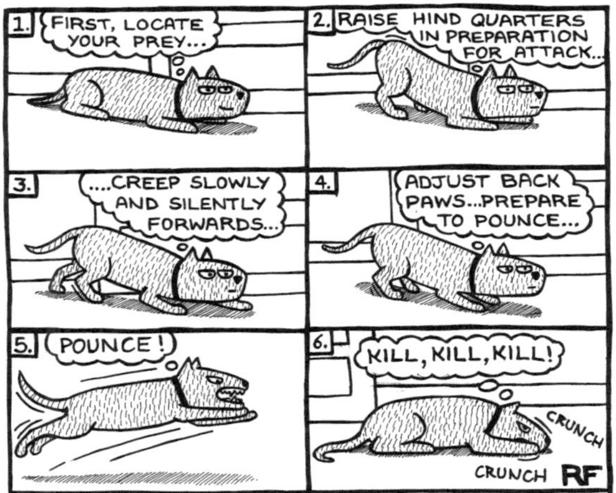

DEATH OF A PING-PONG BALL

MARCH • WEEK 10

monday
6

tuesday
7

wednesday
8

thursday
9

friday
10

saturday
11

○

sunday
12

MARCH

M	T	W	T	F	S	S
		1	2	3	4	5
6	7	8	9	10	11	12
13	14	15	16	17	18	19
20	21	22	23	24	25	26
27	28	29	30	31		

MARCH · WEEK 11

monday 13
Commonwealth Day

tuesday 14

wednesday 15

thursday 16

friday 17
St Patrick's Day
Holiday, Northern Ireland and Republic of Ireland

saturday 18

sunday 19

SCRATCH SCRATCH
OH, YES, DADDY, THAT IS GOOD!
OH, HEAVEN! THIS IS THE BEST!
SCRATCH SCRATCH
YES, YES, YES, YES, YES...
SCRATCH SCRATCH
SCRATCH SCRATCH
PROMISE ME YOU'LL NEVER CUT THOSE FINGER NAILS
SCRATCH SCRATCH
RF

MARCH • WEEK 12

monday
20

Vernal Equinox (Spring begins) ☾

tuesday
21

wednesday
22

thursday
23

friday
24

saturday
25

sunday
26

Mothering Sunday, UK and Republic of Ireland
British Summer Time begins

MARCH

M	T	W	T	F	S	S
		1	2	3	4	5
6	7	8	9	10	11	12
13	14	15	16	17	18	19
20	21	22	23	24	25	26
27	28	29	30	31		

MARCH/APRIL • WEEK 13

monday
27

tuesday
28

wednesday
29

thursday
30

friday
31

saturday
1

sunday
2

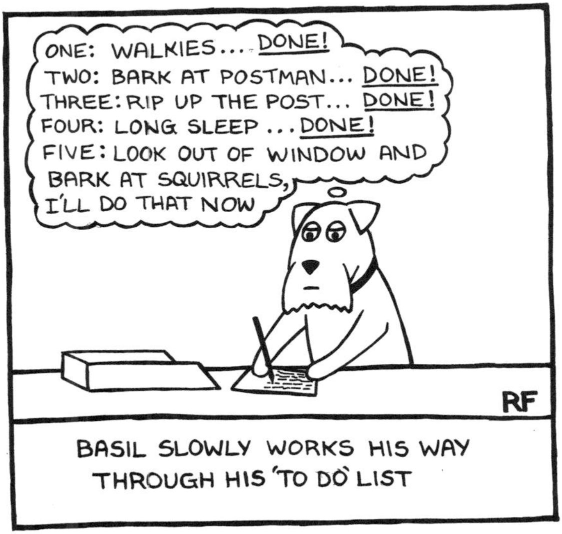

BASIL SLOWLY WORKS HIS WAY THROUGH HIS 'TO DO' LIST

APRIL • WEEK 14

☽

monday
3

tuesday
4

wednesday
5

thursday
6

friday
7

saturday
8

Palm Sunday

sunday
9

APRIL

M	T	W	T	F	S	S
					1	2
3	4	5	6	7	8	9
10	11	12	13	14	15	16
17	18	19	20	21	22	23
24	25	26	27	28	29	30

APRIL · WEEK 15

monday
10

tuesday
11
First day of Passover (Pesach) ○

wednesday
12

thursday
13
Maundy Thursday

friday
14
Good Friday
Holiday, UK, Canada, Australia and New Zealand

saturday
15
Holiday, Australia (Easter Saturday)

sunday
16
Easter Sunday

1
THEY MUST HAVE OVERSLEPT, IT'S MY BREAKFAST TIME!!
2
DONG! DONG! DONG! DONG!
3
DONG! DONG! DONG! DONG!
4
ALRIGHT, ALRIGHT, WE'RE AWAKE! STOP BANGING!
I LOVE THIS RADIATOR!
RF

APRIL • WEEK 16

monday 17 — Easter Monday
Holiday, UK (exc. Scotland), Republic of Ireland, Australia and New Zealand

tuesday 18

wednesday 19 ☾

thursday 20

friday 21 — Birthday of Queen Elizabeth II

saturday 22

sunday 23 — St George's Day

APRIL

M	T	W	T	F	S	S
					1	2
3	4	5	6	7	8	9
10	11	12	13	14	15	16
17	18	19	20	21	22	23
24	25	26	27	28	29	30

APRIL • WEEK 17

monday
24

tuesday
25
Holiday, Australia and New Zealand (Anzac Day)

wednesday
26
●

thursday
27

friday
28

saturday
29

sunday
30

OH, HEAVENS! MY BEST LITTLE BLACK DRESS, COVERED WITH WHITE DOG HAIR!
2.
SCHLIP
SCHLIP
SCHLIP
SCHLIP
SCHLIP
3.
THAT'S BETTER
4.
RF

MAY · WEEK 18

monday
1

Early Spring Bank Holiday, UK
Holiday, Republic of Ireland

tuesday
2

wednesday
3

☽

thursday
4

friday
5

saturday
6

sunday
7

MAY

M	T	W	T	F	S	S
1	2	3	4	5	6	7
8	9	10	11	12	13	14
15	16	17	18	19	20	21
22	23	24	25	26	27	28
29	30	31				

MAY · WEEK 19

monday
8

tuesday
9

wednesday
10 ○

thursday
11

friday
12

saturday
13

sunday
14

Mother's Day, USA, Canada, Australia and New Zealand

SOMEBODY HAS JUMPED ON TO THE KITCHEN TABLE AND EATEN MY SPONGE CAKE!
WELL, WELL, I WONDER WHO THAT COULD HAVE BEEN?
HE, HE, THEY'LL NEVER FIND ME UNDER HERE
RF

MAY · WEEK 20

monday
15

tuesday
16

wednesday
17

thursday
18

friday
19 ☾

saturday
20

sunday
21

MAY

M	T	W	T	F	S	S
1	2	3	4	5	6	7
8	9	10	11	12	13	14
15	16	17	18	19	20	21
22	23	24	25	26	27	28
29	30	31				

MAY · WEEK 21

monday 22 — Holiday, Canada (Victoria Day)

tuesday 23

wednesday 24

thursday 25 — Ascension Day ●

friday 26

saturday 27 — First day of Ramadân (subject to sighting of the moon)

sunday 28

SCRATCH SCRATCH
I ALWAYS SAY, 'IF THERE'S ROOM FOR ONE....
...THERE'S ROOM FOR TWO'
RF

MAY/JUNE • WEEK 22

monday 29 — Spring Bank Holiday, UK / Holiday, USA (Memorial Day)

tuesday 30

wednesday 31 — Feast of Weeks (Shavuot)

thursday 1 — ☽

friday 2 — Queen Elizabeth II's Coronation Anniversary

saturday 3

sunday 4 — Whit Sunday

JUNE

M	T	W	T	F	S	S
				1	2	3	4
5	6	7	8	9	10	11
12	13	14	15	16	17	18
19	20	21	22	23	24	25
26	27	28	29	30		

JUNE • WEEK 23

monday 5
Holiday, Republic of Ireland
Holiday, New Zealand (The Queen's Birthday)

tuesday 6

wednesday 7

thursday 8

friday 9
○

saturday 10
Queen Elizabeth II's Official Birthday
(subject to confirmation)

sunday 11
Trinity Sunday

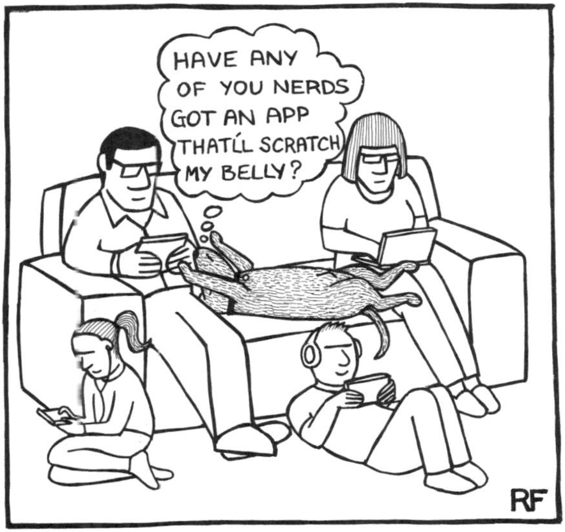
HAVE ANY OF YOU NERDS GOT AN APP THAT'LL SCRATCH MY BELLY?
RF

JUNE · WEEK 24

monday 12 — Holiday, Australia (The Queen's Birthday)

tuesday 13

wednesday 14

thursday 15 — Corpus Christi

friday 16

saturday 17 ☽

sunday 18 — Father's Day, UK, Republic of Ireland, USA and Canada

JUNE

M	T	W	T	F	S	S
			1	2	3	4
5	6	7	8	9	10	11
12	13	14	15	16	17	18
19	20	21	22	23	24	25
26	27	28	29	30		

JUNE · WEEK 25

monday
19

tuesday
20

wednesday
21

Summer Solstice (Summer begins)

thursday
22

friday
23

saturday
24

●

sunday
25

Eid al-Fitr (end of Ramadân)
(subject to sighting of the moon)

A QUIET NIGHT IN FRONT OF THE TV...

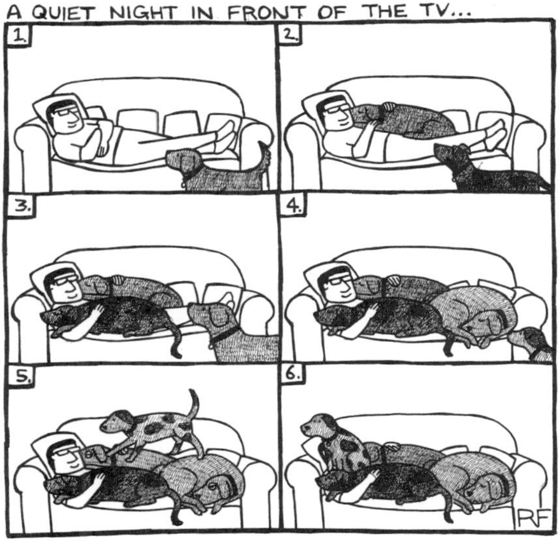

JUNE/JULY • WEEK 26

monday
26

tuesday
27

wednesday
28

thursday
29

friday
30

saturday
1

Canada Day ☽

sunday
2

JULY

M	T	W	T	F	S	S
					1	2
3	4	5	6	7	8	9
10	11	12	13	14	15	16
17	18	19	20	21	22	23
24	25	26	27	28	29	30
31						

JULY • WEEK 27

monday 3 — Holiday, Canada (Canada Day)

tuesday 4 — Holiday, USA (Independence Day)

wednesday 5

thursday 6

friday 7

saturday 8

sunday 9 — ○

SUMMER IS HERE AT LAST...
AHH, YES, SUMMER...TOO HOT TO DO ANYTHING EXCEPT LIE AROUND ALL DAY SNOOZING AND SLEEPING
A BIT LIKE WINTER REALLY
RF

JULY · WEEK 28

monday 10

tuesday 11

wednesday 12

Holiday, Northern Ireland (Battle of the Boyne)

thursday 13

friday 14

saturday 15

St Swithin's Day

sunday 16

☾

JULY

M	T	W	T	F	S	S
					1	2
3	4	5	6	7	8	9
10	11	12	13	14	15	16
17	18	19	20	21	22	23
24	25	26	27	28	29	30
31						

JULY · WEEK 29

monday
17

tuesday
18

wednesday
19

thursday
20

friday
21

saturday
22

sunday
23

1
PEEP PEEP PEEP PEEP
2
BLAH BLAH BLAH
TIME TO HAVE SOME FUN!
3
BLAH BLAH BLAH
ROUND..
4
BLAH BLAH BLAH
AND AROUND...
5
BLAH BLAH BLAH
AND AROUND AND AROUND..
6
STOPPIT, RUFUS! THAT'S NOT FUNNY!
YOU ARE SO WRONG!
RF

JULY • WEEK 30

monday
24

tuesday
25

wednesday
26

thursday
27

friday
28

saturday
29

☽

sunday
30

JULY

M	T	W	T	F	S	S
				1	2	
3	4	5	6	7	8	9
10	11	12	13	14	15	16
17	18	19	20	21	22	23
24	25	26	27	28	29	30
31						

JULY/AUGUST • WEEK 31

monday
31

tuesday
1

wednesday
2

thursday
3

friday
4

saturday
5

sunday
6

HIERARCHY OF AN ANIMAL-LOVING FAMILY....

No. 1 MUM	No. 2 THE KIDS
No. 3 THE DOG	No. 4 THE RABBIT
No. 5 THE GOLDFISH	No. 6 DAD

AUGUST · WEEK 32

monday
7

Holiday, Scotland and Republic of Ireland ○

tuesday
8

wednesday
9

thursday
10

friday
11

saturday
12

sunday
13

AUGUST

M	T	W	T	F	S	S
	1	2	3	4	5	6
7	8	9	10	11	12	13
14	15	16	17	18	19	20
21	22	23	24	25	26	27
28	29	30	31			

AUGUST · WEEK 33

monday
14

tuesday
15
☾

wednesday
16

thursday
17

friday
18

saturday
19

sunday
20

THE JOYS OF SUMMER
1. BARKING AT LAWN SPRINKLERS
YAP YAP YAP
2. KIDDYPOOLS
3. COOL FLOOR TILES
4. ICE CREAM SHARING
5. WATER BITING
RF

AUGUST • WEEK 34

monday
21

tuesday
22

wednesday
23

thursday
24

friday
25

saturday
26

sunday
27

AUGUST

M	T	W	T	F	S	S
	1	2	3	4	5	6
7	8	9	10	11	12	13
14	15	16	17	18	19	20
21	22	23	24	25	26	27
28	29	30	31			

AUGUST/SEPTEMBER • WEEK 35

monday
28

Summer Bank Holiday, UK (exc. Scotland)

tuesday
29

☽

wednesday
30

thursday
31

friday
1

saturday
2

sunday
3

Father's Day, Australia and New Zealand

THIS IS RIDICULOUS. I CAN HARDLY BREATHE
DOGS TODAY
THAAAAATS BETTER
RF

SEPTEMBER · WEEK 36

monday
4
Holiday, USA (Labor Day)
Holiday, Canada (Labour Day)

tuesday
5

wednesday
6
○

thursday
7

friday
8

saturday
9

sunday
10

SEPTEMBER

M	T	W	T	F	S	S
				1	2	3
4	5	6	7	8	9	10
11	12	13	14	15	16	17
18	19	20	21	22	23	24
25	26	27	28	29	30	

SEPTEMBER · WEEK 37

monday
11

tuesday
12

wednesday
13

☾

thursday
14

friday
15

saturday
16

sunday
17

NEW PUPPIES — THE FIRST WEEK...
WE NEED TO MAKE IT CLEAR FROM THE START — NO DOGS ALLOWED ON THE SOFA!
I TOTALLY AGREE
SIX MONTHS LATER...
RF

SEPTEMBER · WEEK 38

monday
18

tuesday
19

wednesday
20

thursday
21

Jewish New Year (Rosh Hashanah)

friday
22

Autumnal Equinox (Autumn begins)
Islamic New Year

saturday
23

sunday
24

SEPTEMBER

M	T	W	T	F	S	S
				1	2	3
4	5	6	7	8	9	10
11	12	13	14	15	16	17
18	19	20	21	22	23	24
25	26	27	28	29	30	

SEPTEMBER/OCTOBER • WEEK 39

monday
25

tuesday
26

wednesday
27

☽

thursday
28

Michaelmas Day

friday
29

Day of Atonement (Yom Kippur)

saturday
30

sunday
1

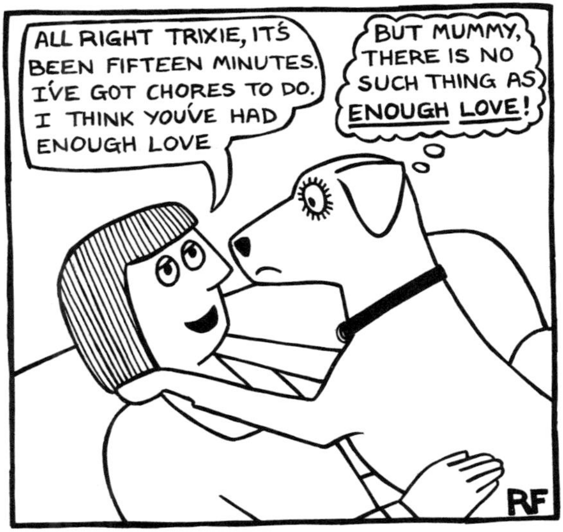

ALL RIGHT TRIXIE, IT'S BEEN FIFTEEN MINUTES. I'VE GOT CHORES TO DO. I THINK YOU'VE HAD ENOUGH LOVE
BUT MUMMY, THERE IS NO SUCH THING AS ENOUGH LOVE!
RF

OCTOBER • WEEK 40

monday
2

tuesday
3

wednesday
4

thursday
5

First day of Tabernacles (Succoth) ○

friday
6

saturday
7

sunday
8

OCTOBER

M	T	W	T	F	S	S
						1
2	3	4	5	6	7	8
9	10	11	12	13	14	15
16	17	18	19	20	21	22
23	24	25	26	27	28	29
30	31					

OCTOBER · WEEK 41

monday
9 — Holiday, USA (Columbus Day)
Holiday, Canada (Thanksgiving)

tuesday
10

wednesday
11

thursday
12 ☾

friday
13

saturday
14

sunday
15

YAY! IT'S SUNDAY! WE CAN SPEND ALL DAY LYING AROUND SLEEPING, SNOOZING AND CHILLIN' OUT!
A BIT LIKE MONDAY, TUESDAY, WEDNESDAY, THURSDAY, FRIDAY AND SATURDAY REALLY!
RF

OCTOBER • WEEK 42

monday
16

tuesday
17

wednesday
18

thursday
19

friday
20

saturday
21

sunday
22

OCTOBER

M	T	W	T	F	S	S
						1
2	3	4	5	6	7	8
9	10	11	12	13	14	15
16	17	18	19	20	21	22
23	24	25	26	27	28	29
30	31					

OCTOBER • WEEK 43

monday
23
                Holiday, New Zealand (Labour Day)

tuesday
24

wednesday
25

thursday
26

friday
27
    ☽

saturday
28

sunday
29
    British Summer Time ends

GIVE MUMMY-WUMMY A CUDDLE-WUDDLE, MY OOTCHIE-COOTCHIE-SMOOTCHIE-POOTCHIE POODLEKINS
I LOVE YOU SOOO MUCH, MY DARLING, CHEEKY-WEEKY CUTEY-PUTEY, POM-POM, CUDDLEMUNCHKIN!
HUGGLE-WUGGLE, SHNUGGLE-BUGGLE, SHNOOZLE-WOOZLE, MY HONEYKINS-BUMPKIN!
SHMOOZY-WHOOZY OOTCHIE COOTCHIE-POOTCHIE, POM-POMS
TO THINK SHE'S AN INTELLIGENT CAREER WOMAN
RF

OCTOBER/NOVEMBER • WEEK 44

monday
30

Holiday, Republic of Ireland

tuesday
31

Halloween

wednesday
1

All Saints' Day

thursday
2

friday
3

saturday
4

○

sunday
5

Guy Fawkes

NOVEMBER

M	T	W	T	F	S	S
		1	2	3	4	5
6	7	8	9	10	11	12
13	14	15	16	17	18	19
20	21	22	23	24	25	26
27	28	29	30			

NOVEMBER · WEEK 45

monday
6

tuesday
7

wednesday
8

thursday
9

friday
10

Holiday, USA (Veterans Day) ☾

saturday
11

Veterans Day, USA
Remembrance Day, Canada

sunday
12

Remembrance Sunday

NOW WHAT DO YOU WANT, ARCHIE?! I'VE SMOTHERED YOU WITH LOVE AND ATTENTION AND AFFECTION AND ADORING HUGS AND STROKES AND CUDDLES AND KISSES ALL MORNING!
IT WASN'T ENOUGH!
RF

NOVEMBER • WEEK 46

monday
13

tuesday
14

wednesday
15

thursday
16

friday
17

saturday
18

sunday
19

NOVEMBER

M	T	W	T	F	S	S
		1	2	3	4	5
6	7	8	9	10	11	12
13	14	15	16	17	18	19
20	21	22	23	24	25	26
27	28	29	30			

NOVEMBER • WEEK 47

monday
20

tuesday
21

wednesday
22

thursday
23
Holiday, USA (Thanksgiving)

friday
24

saturday
25

sunday
26
☽

THE MEALTIME STARE...

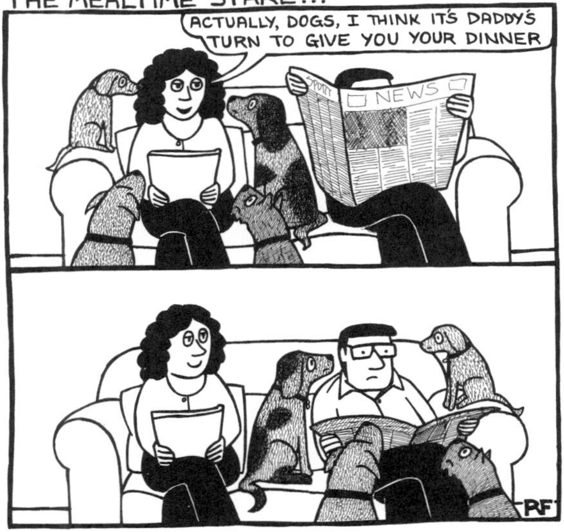

NOVEMBER/DECEMBER • WEEK 48

monday
27

tuesday
28

wednesday
29

thursday
30
St Andrew's Day

friday
1

saturday
2

sunday
3
First Sunday in Advent ○

DECEMBER

M	T	W	T	F	S	S
				1	2	3
4	5	6	7	8	9	10
11	12	13	14	15	16	17
18	19	20	21	22	23	24
25	26	27	28	29	30	31

DECEMBER • WEEK 49

monday
4

tuesday
5

wednesday
6

thursday
7

friday
8

saturday
9

☾

sunday
10

!
STROKE STROKE
IN ORDER TO MAINTAIN A HAPPY AND HARMONIOUS HOUSEHOLD...
...IT IS ESSENTIAL THAT EVERYONE GETS...
...AN EQUAL SHARE OF THE LOVE
STROKE STROKE
RF

DECEMBER · WEEK 50

monday
11

tuesday
12

Hannukah begins (at sunset)

wednesday
13

thursday
14

friday
15

saturday
16

sunday
17

DECEMBER

M	T	W	T	F	S	S
				1	2	3
4	5	6	7	8	9	10
11	12	13	14	15	16	17
18	19	20	21	22	23	24
25	26	27	28	29	30	31

DECEMBER · WEEK 51

monday
18

tuesday
19

wednesday
20
Hannukah ends

thursday
21
Winter Solstice (Winter begins)

friday
22

saturday
23

sunday
24
Christmas Eve

THE S.W.A.T. TEAM...
LOOK! WE HAVE AN INTRUDER! WHITE MALE, FIVE FOOT TALL, APPROX 180 POUNDS. TRILBY HAT
ROGER THAT! LET'S GET DOWN THERE AND TAKE HIM OUT!
YAP YAP YAP YAP YAP
YAP YAP YAP YAP YAP
RF

DECEMBER • WEEK 52

monday
25

Christmas Day
Holiday, UK, Republic of Ireland, USA, Canada,
Australia and New Zealand

tuesday
26

Boxing Day (St Stephen's Day)
Holiday, UK, Republic of Ireland, Canada,
Australia and New Zealand ☽

wednesday
27

thursday
28

friday
29

saturday
30

sunday
31

New Year's Eve

AHA! THE CHRISTMAS PRESENTS! I WONDER WHICH ONE IS MY NEW RUBBER CHICKEN?
SOCKS... AFTERSHAVE.. ... MOBILE PHONE...
RIP RIP RIP
..GLOVES...A BOOK...DVD... ...WALLET... YAY! MY RUBBER CHICKEN!
RIP, RIP, RIP
HA, HA... I LOVE THE WAY THEY WRAPPED ALL THOSE DECOY PRESENTS JUST TO CONFUSE ME
RF

JANUARY • WEEK 1 2018

monday 1 — New Year's Day
Holiday, UK, Republic of Ireland, USA, Canada, Australia and New Zealand

tuesday 2 — Holiday, Scotland and New Zealand   ○

wednesday 3

thursday 4

friday 5

saturday 6 — Epiphany

sunday 7

JANUARY 2018

M T W T F S S

1 2 3 4 5 6 7
8 9 10 11 12 13 14
15 16 17 18 19 20 21
22 23 24 25 26 27 28
29 30 31

HEY ROCKY! GREAT NEWS! THEY'VE BOTH GOT REALLY BAD HANGOVERS!
BRILLIANT! YOU DO THE SQUEAKY TOY AND I'LL DO THE PRETEND SQUIRREL IN THE GARDEN!
WHOA! WHOA! WHOA! WHOA! WHOA!
WHOA! WHOA!
WHOA! WHOA! WHOA!
WHOA! WHOA! WHOA!
NO!
NO!
SQUEAK! SQUEAK! SQUEAK!
SQUEAK! SQUEAK! SQUEAK!
RF

I DON'T BELIEVE IT!! I'M GONNA HAVE TO TAKE THE DOGS FOR MORE WALKS!
RF

THE END